End Time Prophecies

Pastor/Evangelist Barbara Lynch

Words From Her Father Volume 2

Copyright © *2018*
Pastor/Evangelist Barbara Lynch

All rights reserved. No part of this publication may be reproduced, distributed, or transmitted in any form or by any means, including photocopying, recording, or other electronic or mechanical methods, without the prior written permission of the publisher, except in the case of brief quotations embodied in critical reviews and certain other noncommercial uses permitted by copyright law.

Living Bible (TLB)
The Living Bible copyright © 1971 by Tyndale House Foundation. Used by permission of Tyndale House Publishers Inc., Carol Stream, Illinois 60188. All rights reserved.

New International Version (NIV)
Holy Bible, New International Version®, NIV® Copyright ©1973, 1978, 1984, 2011 by Biblica, Inc.® Used by permission. All rights reserved worldwide..

New King James Version (NKJV)
Scripture taken from the New King James Version®. Copyright © 1982 by Thomas Nelson. Used by permission. All rights reserved.

The Message (MSG)
Copyright © 1993, 1994, 1995, 1996, 2000, 2001, 2002 by Eugene H. Peterson

ISBN 13: 978-0-9861572-5-7
ISBN 10: 0-9861572-5-2

Contact the Author:
Light-Bearer Publishing Company
Attn: Pastor Barbara B. Lynch
1458 Parkers Chapel Road
Marydel, DE 19964
barbaralynch@lighthousechurchinc.org

For more prophetic words, to be fed fresh manna from Heaven, and to grow deeper in your walk with God visit: www.lighthousechurchinc.org

Also available in E-book or paperback:

From the Potter's Heart: Words From Her Father Volume 1
Powerful Prophetic Words From The Throne Of Grace

Dedication

To my Heavenly Father,
my Savior and First Love, Jesus Christ,
and my Beloved Companion, the Holy Spirit
to You be all the Glory

Contents

Copyright © 2018 ii

Contact the Author: iii

Dedication iv

Note to the Reader 1

(Section I) INTRODUCTION… 2

(Section I) WARNINGS… 4

   Do Not Wait For the Last Call 4

   Great Falling Away – Judgment 7

   Much Destruction on all Sides 8

   Signs In The Skies 10

   Woe to Those Who Have Not Heeded My True Words 11

   Sorrow and Warfare 15

   Feeling the Wrath Being Poured Out 17

   The Blood is Crying out for Revenge 18

   Fireworks- Signs, Miracles, and Wonders 19

   I Will Devastate This Whole Earth (Also in Section III) 20

   I Keep Warning and Warning (Also in Section III) 22

   America Will Repent (Also in Section III) 23

(Section II) EARTHQUAKES… 24

   Much Devastation: - {THE} Earthquake 24

   Mighty Earthquake 26

   Thunder, Lightning, and Earthquakes 27

   Great Gnashing of Teeth 27

There Will be… Great Earthquakes 28

Revelation 9 – Earthquake Coming (Also in Section III) 29

Worst Devastation in American History (Also in Section III) 32

(Section III) AMERICA… 34

No one Wants to Save the Lost in America 34

WHERE ARE MY CHILDREN? 35

Revival to Sweep Across America 38

America Will no Longer be America 40

Oh America… 41

Much Calamity is Coming upon America 43

Destruction is Coming Upon America 43

Enemy Upon American Soil 45

America bow Your Knee 46

Judgment Upon America 47

Judgment Upon My Beloved America 48

Terror Will Strike America 52

Heavy Hand of Judgment 53

Woe Upon Woe Upon This Land 54

America – Judgment - My Great Wrath 55

Getting America's Undivided Attention 56

Great Explosion -Not End Until it is Finished 57

Sorrow is About to Sweep Across This Nation 57

Great Revival 58

Delaware Revival 59

America and Marriages 60

America is Having… A Great Visitation 62

So Much Trauma Hitting America 64

A Great Time of Unrest 64

I Have Come to America 65

I Keep Warning and Warning (Also in Section I) 65

I Will Devastate This Whole Earth (Also in Section I) 66

America Will Repent (Also in Section I) 68

Worst Devastation in American History (Also in Section II) 69

Revelation 9 – Earthquake Coming (Also in Section II) 69

Aftershock of Sin 72

Conclusion 75

About Pastor/Evangelist Barbara Lynch 76

Note to the Reader

I challenge anyone who sits under the ministry that God has given me to be a well-rounded Christian. You cannot take the parts of the Word of God that you don't like and chuck them aside. You must apply all of it to your everyday existence. For years leaders in Churches have shunned teaching their people the "Full Gospel" If you are serious about Revival you will take into yourself the entire counsel of God.

This book shares the judgments of God for two purposes. Purpose one: so that we all can take part in interceding before God to bring about Revival. Purpose two: so that the "Sinning saints" would come to the knowledge of the Truth that God's grace for the Church has ended. It is past time to get right with the Father. You must get right and stay right. Or you are guaranteed to hear, "Depart from Me you worker of iniquity, I never knew you!"

INTRODUCTION...

No one gets a thrill out the judgments of God; however, if you are to know God's heartbeat you have to make a commitment to know all of His heart. As a prophet I must speak every word that God gives me to speak to the peoples.

A long time ago, I gave my Father permission to speak through me in any way that He saw fit. What I am about to share with you are some of those prophetic words of warning that God has given me for the Body of Christ. I allow Him to use me and He does just that. These are words that God has given me over the past twenty years.

These words focus on three areas. Words of warning, words about the earthquakes and words about the destruction that could come to America if we don't humble ourselves and pray. Some of these prophecies you will see repeated across multiple sections. I wanted to show you the seriousness of what God is saying and how we must line ourselves up with Him.

God has taken me to Hell three times and on each occasion I got a firm understanding of why no one should go there. If these warnings will keep someone from making their home in Hell, then the ridicule and suffering that will come from releasing this book will be worth it all.

No, I am not crazy, I just love my Father and He loves me. I am excited about being in fellowship with the creator of the world. I look forward to spending time with Him in eternity but for now my task is not yet completed. We must bring in the harvest in cooperation with Christ. Night is coming and pretty soon no man will be able to work.

Do not **ignore** these warnings from the Lord. He cares enough to send His messengers, the angels and another non-demonic messengers, **His prophets**, your way. All to bring you out of darkness into His marvelous light. Take these warnings seriously. Don't ignore these prophetic warnings, because only God can stop the destruction that is coming our way.

(Section I) WARNINGS…

Do Not Wait For the Last Call

My children, I am a God of **resurrection power**. And I have come (even this night) to resurrect that which the enemy has destroyed. The palmer and the canker worm have come and have stolen **everything** that I have given you. He has utterly destroyed all of my promises in each one of your lives.

But I the Lord thy God, I say to you this night, that as you set your faces as flint before Me; and as you yield yourself totally and completely to Me, the Living and True God, **I will resurrect all that is dead**. I will bring it all back to life and it will be life, more abundantly.

I have spoken in My word that **I would give you beauty for ashes**; and I have also said that I would take you from glory to glory to glory.

I am going to rapture you up into My bosom; and I am going to do great and mighty things in you and through you. I am going to manifest My power like no other has seen --- for this is truly the day of resurrection; This is truly the day that the enemy must stop his onslaught against My chosen people.

The enemy is raging. Leviathan has raised his head over and over and over again. But I say that as you stay before Me; Stay in My presence; My Holy Angels will be sent forth to destroy every leviathan that raises up his ugly head.

I have spoken and so shall it be.

I am truly not a man that I should lie. What I have spoken shall surely come to pass.

There are many lives on the forefront at this given hour. There are many in My kingdom who have played the harlot, and now their lives lay in complete and total devastation.

But I, the Lord thy God, I promise that as you hold these lives up before Me, that I am able to come in, and I am able to **correct** what the canker worm and the palmer worm has done.

I am able to restore to wholeness all of My people who truly **call upon My name and repent before Me the True and Living God.**

The answer is **not to quit**; but the answer is to **press forward** as you never pressed forward before. The answer is to hold on to My everlasting arms as you have never held onto them before.

You need to read about the martyrs in the days past, how they did not think of their lives, but all they thought about was one day sitting at My feet in the heavenly throne room.

They suffered much persecution for My name's sake. They gave up their lives willingly, knowing that they had a far better reward in heaven then they had in this earth.

So, My children, know that I have come, and I have spoken in your midst this night, and that I have promised you that I am the **Resurrection King,** and I will resurrect all that has died.

Stand on the **sure foundation**. Stand on the **rock that cannot be moved**. And you will see victory on every side. You will see **true victory** on every side.

Rise up this night --- come forward in Me --- and know that I, the True and Living God, I am for you and not against you --- and that I am arraying **a host of heavenly angels** around about you, even this very second, and that host of heavenly angels will keep you safe from all harm.

Those who are playing the harlot in My house, I give notice this night I do not condone it, I will never condone it and I have already brought My judgment against it.

So My children, **stand firm** and **stand fast** knowing that I, the Lord thy God, I am moving throughout the Body of Christ; I am separating the wheat from the chaff; and I have already brought My **judgment** into the house.

But know this night, what I have promised you, and what the canker worm has stolen; **I have come by this way tonight to tell you that I will resurrect it**. So rest at my feet and know that I am the True and Living God, and I do not lie.

{*Word of Knowledge*} **Many are missing the opportunity to touch the hem of His garment.** *You're by passing the hem of His garment, and you have to touch the hem of His garment.* **That is faith.** *Faith reaches out and touches the hem of His garment; and faith says Lord, you can do it all!*

There is no mountain too big, and no mountain too small, that I cannot remove.

You have to touch the hem of His garment with your faith before the mountains will ever go away. This is My final call for My children.

{*Word of Knowledge*} *We think in a service, when God says -- I am not coming by again -- we think that is the night, but that is not really how it works. But this is truly His final call to His children, and one day He is going to close the door to that call and then you will knock and He will not open it again. So everybody needs to hearken unto the* **final call** *that God has given -- for* **total surrender** *--* **total purity** *and* **total holiness** *before a Holy God.*

Great Falling Away – Judgment

There are very few that will set by My side in this hour little one, so be prepared for a great falling away of the Body of Christ.

Many are the afflictions of the righteous, and many will fall away because they will not be able to endure the afflictions. They falsely believe that just because they follow Me, that all will be well, but not so.

There is nowhere in My word that I said My people would **not** be persecuted, for My names sake. But the lies have been spoken and the truth was not revealed to a generation that would not take up their sword and follow Me.

They trusted in man, and now man has failed them and they do not know where to turn. But I am raising up a generation that will only know Me and only follow Me. I will put My word deep into their bosom and I will do a great and mighty works through them.

Many transgressions have been performed in My house, in the name of the Lord, and I am coming to rectify those transgressions. Few will be able to take the chastening rod, and the rest will fall away.

I am a loving Father, and I have asked My people over and over again to come and have sweet fellowship with Me, but to no avail. They think I am a foreign Father, that does not watch over his children, but all will know that I do watch over My children and I do watch over My word to perform it. At the given time, I will cause

My Word to come into fruition. But not until the proper given time will this come into being.

Many souls are being weighed in the balance and have come up wanting. I have held back My chastening rod for a season, to give them time to repent and come into My Everlasting Arms and be healed of their pain, guilt and condemnation. But soon that window will be closed and I will open another window of chastisement.

Do not be taken aback at what you will see in the following days, because I am about to unleash My Glory and when My Glory falls, many souls will be brought into the Kingdom and many more in the house of God will be freed from their prison houses. I am just asking you to stand still and see the salvation of the Lord at work on your behalf. Be still little one, be still in the midst of these great storms that are not on the horizon any longer, but they have come upon the land and they are wreaking great havoc amongst My people.

The cup of wrath is being poured out at this given time and many will feel the effects of a righteous judge. The winds of adversity are truly blowing and many do not understand the full effects of these winds, but they will!

Much Destruction on all Sides

I was dressing this morning and started to cry uncontrollably. I came into the computer room and started crying out to God and this is what I heard:

My heart weeps for My house, for My house will not hear My pleas for repentance. My sorrow goes so deep. My heart breaks at every turn.

Why children? Why won't you turn to Me with your whole heart? Why does the world have such a pull upon you and your families? I have pondered over this for ages, and I have only one answer. The world holds more for your heart than I do, so you think!

The wages of war are so costly. But the wars must come now, for My people would not repent and turn from their wicked evil ways. These wars will cost you more than you care to pay.

There will be great wailing and gnashing of teeth heard on the streets. For the soon coming despair will outweigh anything that the world has ever experienced.

Many will bemoan the very day they were born. The homosexual community will be destroyed. I will not be mocked. I am not a bastard. I am the true Father of all creation.

Why do you, church, think the enemy created? Why do you think he is in control? You will soon see who is in control, and for some it will be too late, for others, they will finally see that all I have spoken is coming to pass and they will fall upon their faces in total worship of a loving and caring Father.

Hold tight to what you have in Me, church! Hold tight, for it will be worth it all in the very end.

Much destruction on all sides - Many will be running to and fro, and many will be seeking places of refuge, but will be unable to find any. Total disaster awaits this world as you see it.

I am not a God of destruction, but I do destroy when necessary. As you read My Word, you will see destruction after destruction and devastation on all sides. This was because My people refused to follow My voice.

I sent My Son, so His blood would be atonement for sins, but even that has been trampled underfoot. I am left with no alternative, but to bring destruction, so I can rebuild My world once again.

Woe upon woe. Sorrow on all sides. But I will be with My

remnant in all this. You who have chosen Me in the years past have chosen a good thing, all those who chose the things of the world will reap what they have sown.

Go Church and preach My gospel to a lost and dying world. For My Son will soon return for a glorious church, one without spot nor wrinkle.

I ask you to abide under the shadow of the Almighty until My Son's soon return.

Signs In The Skies

There is no time like the present to be looking unto Me, the author and finisher of your life. I have spoken through My prophets since time began, and I am still speaking through My prophets. I am also speaking through My Word, and through the Signs in the sky.

Look around about you. What do you see?

Wars and rumors of wars. Fighting on every front. My people running to and fro seeking understand and finding none.

Is it not time to stop running to and fro and begin to sit at My feet and receive understanding from Me? After all, it is I that created this earth and it is I that is going to bring My son back to this earth.

The peoples are looking unto themselves and they are forgetting about Me, the true and living God. What a shame. My people perish from lack of knowledge and there is no excuse for it, for My Word is full of knowledge and understanding. I have given My people eyes to see and ears to hear, but they are not seeing nor are they comprehending what I am saying at this given time.

It is exposure time and I am exposing all that is darkness

throughout this land.

It is revelation time and I am revealing Myself to all that desire to know more of Me. It is heart-rendering time and all who rend their hearts and not their garments, I will in no wise cast out.

Many teachers, but no truth. I am demanding truth to be spoken to My people and all those who will not reveal the truth of My Word to the peoples shall be done away with. For I will have My truth preached through out this land.

There are many perishing, and where are the teachers of truth? Are they in some obscure place, where no one can hear them? No they are right before your very eyes, but My church has hardened her heart to the truth and they will not receive the truth. But the day is coming and is now upon the land, where My truth shall prevail all across this land.

Lightning and thunder shall proceed out of the mouths of My prophets and they shall surely declare the day of the Lord is at hand. Sorrow after sorrow is upon My church, but they shall prevail, for I have brought My Sword and I am cutting all that binds My church.

You shall see Joy and Laughter break out in My church once again as the truth of My Word is given forth, for My word brings life to the very bone and Joy to the very heart.

Do not slumber and sleep, but keep your ears tuned to My voice church and look up, for surely your redemption doth draweth nigh, saith the Lord.

Woe to Those Who Have Not Heeded My True Words

The night is far spent and My children are still not ready for what I have called them forth to do. They are still sitting in their own little places; doing their own little things; not heeding the call- not paying attention to the words that I speak.

What am I to do? What am I to do, but pass over them and bring in the lost and the dying, feed them, nourish them, bring them forth and send them out? I have been calling for years now, to My church to come alive in Me and do the things I have called her forth to do, but to no avail.

Oh yes, there are a few who are trying. There are a few who are standing firm and standing tall, but they are such a small few.

Where is My Body? They are in their own little world, doing their own little things, paying attention to their own little problems and never once doing what I have called them forth to do. And then they wonder why the enemy has a strong hold over their lives. They won't pray. They won't read My Word. They won't come into My house. They just sit in a state of lethargy and expect Me to bless. They judge, they criticize, they condemn. They pass over the ones they think are not worthy and they go to the ones they think are worthy. I want you to know tonight that I am still God and I am still on the throne. And all will stand in total amazement at what they see in the days ahead. For I, the Lord thy God, am going to move. And all will be amazed at how I move, who I use and what I do.

Some are out there prophesying great big things. It is not Me saith the Lord; it is not Me!

I tell you My children, I have called you to total holiness; total commitment and I have not changed My mind.

Why would I allow you to do what I would not allow My Son to do? My Son had to stay in total holiness. My Son had to stand tall and stand firm through all the persecutions. My Son had to fulfill His assignment here on this earth. So why? Why in this world would I ever allow you to do something that I did not allow My Son to do?

I tell you this night; you have not heeded My Word church. You have not heeded My Prophets. And you will soon see that you are in the wrong, but it will be too late. For I am going to pass many by.

Many are called, but few are chosen.

I have called many, many into My Kingdom. I have given them great swelling words of what I desire to do with their lives. But they chose to look over those things and they chose to go ahead and go their own way and do their own thing. They knew that I would use them anyway, but I am not! I am not! Look in My Word. Many I passed by. Many I passed by and went and used another. And I am still the same God today as I was then.

I tell you My church you will see. You will soon see what this is all about. And then for the church it will be too late. But for those who have said: (yes Lord, here am I). For those that I clean up and bring into My house, they will understand Me in all My fullness and they will go forth and do a great and mighty works for Me.

Did I not prophesy of the gross darkness that would cover this earth? Look around about you.

Where is the light? There are not very many lights in this world, but there is much, much darkness.

Too much selfishness. Too much self-centeredness. Too much playing games. That's darkness! And it becomes gross darkness.

Church I say to you this night I have spoken and so shall it be. I will do what I have purposed in My heart to do and there will be no turning back.

The time has come for the great falling away. And the time

has come for the reaping of the harvest. And it is in this harvest that is reaped that I will bring forth My true David's. You will see. You will see.

I have asked you to dance before Me, but you won't dance. I have asked you to praise Me, but you won't praise me. But yet, you will go to the enemy and let him use you and you will bow to him at every turn. You will do whatever he commands and asks you to do. Yet you won't even do what I have asked you to do.

Where is there justice in all of this? I ask you tonight, where is there justice in all of this? Why should I bless? Why should I bless, when you have turned your back on Me?

So what if you don't understand what I am doing? Have I not said lean not to your own understanding? Have I not said your ways are not My ways?

Why can't you just trust Me? Why can't you just have faith in Me? And why can't you just do the things I have called you forth to do?

My question tonight is WHY?

You need to check out your own light. How bright is your light?

Some of you must understand this night that your light has grown so dim, that it is not penetrating the darkness at all. It is not doing anything for Me.

Check out your light this night. Check it out. And see how close to going out it truly is.

It used to burn bright, but check it out. Slowly, but surely it has burnt down and it is ready to go out. You must ignite that light once again. You must cause it to shine in a dark, dark world. You must be the one. You must be the one!

I will not bless strife. I will not bless anger. I will not bless the ones who will not love. There are so many things that I am not blessing. But everyone believes that I should pour out My blessings. Check yourself out tonight.

Why should I truly bless you? You have to ask yourself that. You have to be honest with yourself. Why should I truly bless you?

I have asked you to forgive. You won't forgive. I have asked you to love and you pretend to love. I have asked you to be faithful and you won't be faithful.

Why should I bless?

Sorrow and Warfare

This is just the beginning of sorrows for My people. There is much destruction on the horizon and My people are not prepared to meet this destruction. They have prayed and then laid back on their laurels and believe that nothing is going to happen, but the destruction is coming upon the land. Life will go on, but not the same as before.

Many will be running to and fro and they will not be able to find peace, but My true church will know Me **as the center of peace** and they will lead the others to the place of peace that only abides within Me. I have asked My people to come out from under the mundane and walk in the supernatural, but they are refusing to do so.

Time will tell! Time will tell on those who would not heed My warnings and all will finally see that I truly did speak and warn My church, but to no avail.

The time of great warfare is upon this land and you (church) must war as never before. You must come to the throne of grace as never before. You must stay at the altar of incense as never before and you must come out victorious on all sides. I have spoken and so shall it be, saith the Lord.

Warfare! Warfare! Warfare on all sides and only those who have been trained to walk in My circumference of safety will make it through this terrible hour of great warfare that has come upon this land

Marshall law will now come into effect. You will see destruction on every side.

Many suicides will occur at this given time. Many will walk in fear for their very lives. But I have warned and I have warned, but to no avail.

Now My true church will emerge upon the scene with signs, wonders and miracles and they shall bring peace in the midst of this chaotic world.

Be still and know that I am God and fight the good fight of faith and prevail at all cost.

> **Exodus 30: 1-10 (NIV)**
> "Make an altar of acacia wood for burning incense. It is to be square, a cubit long and a cubit wide, and two cubits high—its horns of one piece with it. Overlay the top and all the sides and the horns with pure gold, and make a gold molding around it. Make two gold rings for the altar below the molding—two on each of the opposite sides—to hold the poles used to carry it. Make the poles of acacia wood and overlay them with gold. Put the altar in front of the curtain that shields the ark of the covenant law—before the atonement cover that is over the tablets of the covenant law—where I will meet with you.

"Aaron must burn fragrant incense on the altar every morning when he tends the lamps. He must burn incense again when he lights the lamps at twilight so incense will burn regularly before the Lord for the generations to come. Do not offer on this altar any other incense or any burnt offering or grain offering, and do not pour a drink offering on it. Once a year Aaron shall make atonement on its horns. This annual atonement must be made with the blood of the atoning sin offering for the generations to come. It is most holy to the Lord."

Revelation 8: 1-5 (NIV)
When he opened the seventh seal, there was silence in heaven for about half an hour. And I saw the seven angels who stand before God, and seven trumpets were given to them.

Another angel, who had a golden censer, came and stood at the altar. He was given much incense to offer, with the prayers of all God's people, on the golden altar in front of the throne. The smoke of the incense, together with the prayers of God's people, went up before God from the angel's hand. Then the angel took the censer, filled it with fire from the altar, and hurled it on the earth; and there came peals of thunder, rumblings, flashes of lightning and an earthquake.

Romans 12:1-2 (NIV)
Therefore, I urge you, brothers and sisters, in view of God's mercy, to offer your bodies as a living sacrifice, holy and pleasing to God—this is your true and proper worship. Do not conform to the pattern of this world, but be transformed by the renewing of your mind. Then you will be able to test and approve what God's will is—his good, pleasing and perfect will.

Hebrews 13: 10-16 (NIV)
We have an altar from which those who minister at the tabernacle have no right to eat.

The high priest carries the blood of animals into the Most Holy Place as a sin offering, but the bodies are burned outside the camp. And so Jesus also suffered outside the city gate to make the people holy through his own blood. Let us, then, go to him outside the camp, bearing the disgrace he bore. For here we do not have an enduring city, but we are looking for the city that is to come.

Through Jesus, therefore, let us continually offer to God a sacrifice of praise—the fruit of lips that openly profess his name. And do not forget to do good and to share with others, for with such sacrifices God is pleased.

Feeling the Wrath Being Poured Out

Father, what am I feeling?

You are feeling the wrath that is being poured out upon My people. Those who have called Me by name, but refuse to live up to that calling.

I have spoken so many times in the past of this great tribulation that would come upon My children, but no one is listening.

The wars will continue and many will lose their lives, but I must do this thing. It is the end! I am winding everything up, for My Son is anxiously awaiting His second return.

There will be great jubilation in the heavenly realm at the appearance of My saints, but on the other hand there will be great gnashing of teeth on the earth.

Celebrate, daughter celebrate the return of My Son. Let the high praises ring and celebrate the coming of My Son for the second and final time. Little is known of My Son's second coming, for many will not receive this idea. My thoughts are not the thoughts of man and My ways are not the ways of man, but My Spirit has been trying to get man to move by My Spirit, but flesh is so prevalent.

Daughter, the Kingdom of Heaven is at hand, and there is so much work to be done in such a short time. Do not be caught up in the affairs of this world, but keep your ears in tuned to My voice and move with Me, saith your Father.

The Blood is Crying out for Revenge

The sins of this world have come up to the heavenly throne room as a stench to My nostrils. And I am grieved with My people. My prophets are feeling the separation from Me as My Son did when He hung on the cross and all the sins of the world were on His shoulders and I had to turn My back on Him for I cannot look upon sin.

In the days ahead you will see much darkness cover all the earth, for a wave of terrorism is going to come upon this land. And many will run to and fro. And many lives will be lost and many will run to the cross, but still others will remain in their lethargic state. And they will know that I am the God of all the earth. And I am in full and complete control but they will not turn from their wicked evil ways, saith the Lord.

Many will fall by the sword in the coming days and many will seek My face for direction, but I have already spoken what direction to go in, but to no avail.

Trouble, trouble, trouble on all sides. Peace will evade many at this given time, because they did not heed the wooing of My Holy Spirit.

Conquer the enemies of your souls My people! Conquer the enemies of your souls before it is too late! I have given all I am going to give. My Son's blood was the atonement for sins, but you trampled that blood underfoot and now the blood is crying out for revenge.

Fireworks- Signs, Miracles, and Wonders

The earth as My people know it, soon will not be. For I am going to transform this earth into the image that I foreordained it to be. Some will stand in total awe, while others will shout the victory, for they have been awaiting this day for a long time.

Now is My hour of great visitation upon this whole earth. Now is the time of the Great Signs, Wonders and Miracles that I have spoke of in My word. This is My churches hour to shine like never before.

This is the hour for My church to rise up and see the fullness of My Glory cover all the earth. This end time revelation of My Glory will surely open the eyes that were once blinded by the darkness and many shall run to My footstool and take up their cross and follow Me.

I am not a burdensome Father. I am a Father that loves His children and only wants what is best for them. I am about to do the Fourth of July that I have prophesied about so many times. The fireworks will be soon throughout the nations. Many will come and dine at the table that I have set before them, and they will eat fresh manna from the heavenly throne room.

Signs, wonders and miracles will be only the beginning of what I am about to do throughout this earth. Whole nations will come to the cross in one day. Multitudes that have been in the valley of decision will rise up overnight and run to the saving grace of a loving heavenly Father. They will know no lack. For they shall be filled with My glory as the great apostles that went before them.

Take heed lest any should fall and come short of My glory.

1 Corinthians 10:12 (NIV)
So, if you think you are standing firm, be careful that you

don't fall!

Romans 3:23 (NIV)
For all have sinned and fall short of the glory of God

{Vision} **At this point**, God showed me **heat**. I asked the Father what that was and He said it was the heat coming from the fire that He was placing (in His Apostles bosoms) and they would carry a word of repentance that would bring multitudes to His Kingdom.

Then I saw rain. I asked the Father what the rain was and He said it was the former and the latter rain that He spoke of in Joel and it would cover the earth and many would be saved and do great exploits for Him.

I Will Devastate This Whole Earth (Also in Section III)

There are mountains and then there ARE MOUNTAINS! I am calling you forth at this given time to hurdle over the mountain tops and stay securely rooted and grounded in Me.

I know who I am, but My people do not know who they are and the enemy comes again and again to steal from My chosen people.

When will they learn? How long will it take?

For some it will take so long that it will be too late. For others they are going to wise up quickly and they will arise out of the ash heap and serve Me with all of their hearts.

This is the greatest time of decision in the church history. This decision will make or break My church.

It is time to arise up out of the ash heap and serve the Living

God and serve Him only, for I will have no other Gods before Me. I am true and I am faithful and I fail not My peoples. Look up peoples!

Look up, for your redemption doth truly draw nigh.

Just as quickly as New Orleans was destroyed, I will devastate this whole earth. Many will be running to and fro. The peoples will be about their normal everyday lives and suddenly out of nowhere I will appear and it will be all over. I have spoken this before and nobody heeded My voice. I am <u>speaking</u> it again and still they will not heed My voice.

Destruction must come upon this nation, for they are making themselves a nation without a Father. They are taking Me out of everything and I am wroth with My peoples.

Come and take counsel from Me, saith the Father. Come and take counsel from Me and learn the truth of what is happening round about you. You are transgressing My laws daily and I will not permit it any longer. You have cast Me asunder. You have brought Me to shame over and over again. Enough is enough and I am tired of this horseplay that you call church and I have come to put an end to it.

Take not counsel from the ungodly, for they are already lost. Seek counsel from Me, for I am your counselor. I and only I have the answers to your questions.

Why do you forsake Me over and over again? Why not just come to the throne of grace and accept all that My Son did for you? WHY? That is My question to you tonight. WHY?

I Keep Warning and Warning *(Also in Section III)*

I am speaking volumes, but still nobody is listening. I keep warning and warning and warning, but nobody cares. They think this all a big hoax that will just disappear.

Daughter, when will they ever learn that this is not going to go away. We are at the end time and the gross darkness is surely covering this earth. The election of this presidency (prophecy given in April 2009) opened up the regions of hell to devour My land. Now, the church must fight as never before. They did not seek My face. They did not adhere to the Constitution of the United States of America and now they are being sold to foreign countries. Where are the intercessors? Where are those that will lay out before me on behalf of this once great state?

They are too busy trying to keep it together. There is nothing absolutely nothing that is going to keep it together. It is falling apart and it will continue to fall apart. This is what sin will do for a nation. The slaughterer has surely come and he has unleashed all of his fury upon My Great Nation. But then he had to have an open door to work from and this nation gave him a wide door of opportunity.

Stand back My faithful ones. Stand back and do not get caught up in the slaughter of innocent babies. Stand back and pray without ceasing. I will not stay My hand of wrath, but I will save a multitude of souls as you pray without ceasing. It truly is fasting and prayer time for My faith ones. It is surely time that you take up the sword and go forth destroying the enemy at every turn. Do not look around about you. You already know what is occurring. Just fast and pray. Just fast and pray.

America Will Repent (Also in Section III)

This is My storm and this is My wrath. I have been displeased with this nation for some time now and I have given this nation time to repent, but to no avail. I have run out of time for a lot of things and I must be about My business.

This time of great trouble has been spoken of for years now, but no one would listen. But I will have My way! I will have My way! When all is said and done there will be still many that will not turn to

Me, in fact in the midst of these trials there are many who have already turned their back upon Me and cursed Me. They have sold themselves out to the evil one and there is no turning back.

How much more will I do? You just stand back and watch. There is much more to come and I promise you this.

America will repent and they will turn from their wicked evil ways, but not all.

Church upon church will fall at this given time and will not be rebuilt. For I am purging My ministers and all who will not listen and heed My warnings will be taken out of their ministries.

It has been to long now. It has been to long for the sin to rule and reign in My houses.

Watch what I am about to do in My churches. Watch and see that what I have spoken I am doing. Not about to do, but am doing.

This is the time spoken of in Joel chapter 2. Great tribulation! Great tribulation!

(Section II) EARTHQUAKES...

Much Devastation: - {THE} Earthquake

You shall see the rise and fall of many nations at this given time. There is much discussion going on that is in line with the end time events.

Russia will invade China and then Russia will take over Israel, then at that given time I will rapture up My church and the great tribulation will begin upon this earth.

Many are discussing the end time events, but not all understand the end time events. I am unrolling the scrolls at this very moment and the angels are in position to carry out their given tasks upon the earth.

You will always hear of wars and rumors of war, but keep looking up, for surely the end is at hand.

Many false gods and antichrists will start appearing on the scene at this given time. Much will be said that is not of Me, but I will prevail among My people. I will have the upper hand in all the events at all times.

Much tribulation on all sides. Much, much more destruction

on the horizon. Darkness like has never been seen before. But through it all, I am in full control.

This is the year for no compromise in the Body. This is the year for much success in the Body. This is the year for the fulfillment of all My promises to My children.

The heavens are open wide, just reach up and receive. Receive of Me all that I have promised to you. Oh, just taste and see that I am good. Have I not spoken it? Will it not come to pass? Yes and Amen saith your Father.

The ships have landed. The ships are loaded with wonderful cargo. Find your ship and receive all your cargo, for your ship has come in. Promises, after promises, after promises being fulfilled at this given time.

This is your year of Jubilee. This is your year of great rejoicing with the saints. Rejoice! Rejoice! REJOICE, saith your Father. For I am the all-knowing, all seeing God, and I am blessing beyond your wildest dreams.

Look up, Look up, Look up, it is from the hills that your help cometh. Look up!

You will see calamity on all sides, but it will not touch My chosen elect. The faithful remnant. The faithful ones. They shall come through all this turmoil unscathed. And they shall be rejoicing, for they will have seen the face of the Father. They will know My heartbeat. They will know My ways. They will be cleansed from all iniquity.

But the unfaithful. Oh, the scathing wrath has come down upon them and they shall burn in their indignation. I have spoken and so shall it be, saith the Father.

This is also the year that I am requiring total crucifixion of the flesh. All flesh must die, for flesh cannot stand in My presence. I am an all-consuming God and I will consume all the flesh you yield unto Me, the true and living God.

Great **earthquakes** all over the land. But {THE} earthquake shall come and it will wreak much devastation upon the land. Hurricane, after hurricane will come across the land. They will devour everything in sight.

The locust and the palmerworm will do an utter destruction upon this land. But I have promised My chosen ones that I would restore all that the palmerworm has stolen. Be of good cheer at this given time, for victory is truly for My chosen ones, and they shall not dwell in defeat any longer.

Mighty Earthquake

Thunder and lightning shall proceed out of My Holy Mountain in the few short days ahead. Many shall stand in amazement at what they see. For I am giving My People a sign and a wonder to behold and all will know that it is I, the Lord thy God that is doing this thing.

From My Holy Mountain I am commanding My Holy angels to go forth and do My bidding at this given time. There shall not be one stone left unturned at this given time, for I am about My business of restoration and I am restoring all that the canker and palmer worm has stolen from My chosen generation.

Many sorrows are going to overtake My people in the few short days ahead and all will know that I am not a man that I should lie. Many souls will lie at My feet totally destroyed by the mighty **earthquake** that is coming upon the land at this given time.

Many more souls will run into the house of the Lord and will cry out for repentance. I shall receive them into My bosom and you shall see the floodgates of heaven open wide at this given time and you shall see many restored into My Kingdom.

Much slaughter shall take place in the earthly realm, for the battle has been raging in the heavenly realm and now it is going to manifest itself upon this earth.

The enemy will wreak much havoc across this land. I forewarned My people, but they closed their ears to My prophets and they did not heed My cries of warning that went throughout the land.

Thunder, Lightning, and Earthquakes

I am coming after My people and it shall not be long. I have set time in space and I am moving in My time frame and I am accomplishing all that needs to be done at this given hour to line things up for the second coming of My Son Jesus.

It will be too late for some and there will be great gnashing and wailing of teeth. Many will cry out in anger, but I will not hear their cry, for I have sent My Holy Prophets. I have set the signs in the heavens and they still ignore all that I say and do.

Thunder and lightning's will resound throughout this earth. Great **earthquakes** will occur. All this will happen because of the lining up with My time frame for the great and terrible day of tribulation that is coming upon this land.

Hearts will faint for fear. Many will give in to the heavy weights that satan places around their necks. But I am coming after My Bride. I have been preparing her for a long time and it is time for the great celebration to begin.

Great Gnashing of Teeth

Once again I am going to blow across this land with My Mighty Outpouring of My Holy Spirit. Once again I am going to anoint My people to hear My voice like never before.

Once again I am going to cause My people to dance and rejoice before Me. Once again I am going to blow the trumpet in Zion. Once again I am going to cause My people to rejoice before the King of Kings, and then the great tribulation will begin.

Many signs and wonders will be seen in the heavenlies. Great **earthquakes** will be heard all across this great nation. But the end is not yet. There is an appointed time for the end.

My timing is always right on time. I am not slack in what I have set in motion. At that time there will be great gnashing of teeth.

I am getting ready to jump-start My church once again. My church has been in a state of lethargy long enough now and I am coming after My church. My church will shine in this dark, dark world as I have foreordained it to. Nobody, absolutely nobody will be able to stop My plans that are already set in motion over this earth. You shall see Me move in mysterious ways and you shall know that I have surely come after My church.

There Will be... Great Earthquakes

You are a people who lack spiritual understanding of the end time events that are already upon this Nation.

There will be floods, wars and rumors of wars; great **earthquakes**; tsunamis of all kinds all across the land; devastation after devastation is going to occur and My people will perish for lack of knowledge of these end time events.

The current events are nothing compared to what is coming upon this land. Talking about slaying the giant is mild to what you will slay. My church will slay even the very throes of hell before this event is over.

Multitude after multitude standing in the doorway of decision. Who will go to them with My uncompromised word? Who will stand in the gap with intercessory prayer believing in the awesomeness of their maker?

Who will have faith for victory after victory in this warfare that is already upon this land?

Whom shall I send and whose report are you going to believe.

I have so much in store for the church that can believe in the Supernatural. Who can flow with the anointing of fire that I have already begun to release upon this land?

What else must I do to get you prepared church; for this end time event?

I am standing at the door and knocking; will you let me in?

Isaiah 53:1 (NKJV)
Who has believed our report?
And to whom has the arm of the Lord been revealed?

Isaiah 6:8 (NKJV)
Also I heard the voice of the Lord, saying: "Whom shall I send, and who will go for Us?" Then I said, "Here am I! Send me."

Luke 12:49(NKJV)
"I came to send fire on the earth, and how I wish it were already kindled!

Revelation 9 – Earthquake Coming *(Also in Section III)*

I long for My people who call Me by name to come into the Holy of Holies and worship with Me there. I long for them to come into the place of everlasting Love and Safety. But they will not. They continue to hang around the cesspools of Sodom and Gomorrah and they no longer abide under the shadow of the Almighty, but they continue to go down their own path of destruction.

I am worthy to be praised and I am demanding praise from My people at this given time. All shall see the salvation of the Lord, but to what degree? Will they truly walk in salvation, or will they stand idly by and watch as others go on with Me and they are consumed with the cares and idols of this world?

Only time will tell, and time will surely tell, saith the Father, for I am going to bring it all out into the light. Every dot and every tittle. And all will see that I am God and that I have not forsaken My own. I have shown My hand of wrath, but still My church, the ones that call Me by My name, is still going their own way and confessing that it is I that is leading, guiding and directing them.

Woe upon woe! My words have gone forth and they shall not come back to Me void.

What is left for Me to do? Tell Me, My children, what is left to do.

You have forsaken the one and only living God and you have made your own Gods. You have plowed deep the furloughs of evil and you sow wild seeds continually. Your harvest is now coming forth and it will truly set your teeth on edge, saith the One and Only True God. I have spoken and so shall it be.

Jeremiah 31:30 (NIV)
Instead, everyone will die for their own sin; whoever eats

sour grapes—their own teeth will be set on edge.

Everlasting chains of judgment await those who would not yield to My wooing and My warnings.

I tried to not touch the American shores, but America would not repent entirely and completely. She still holds onto her idols thinking that I will not revenge the blood of My Son that ran down Calvary's hill.

This **earthquake** is another wake up call for America, but what is she doing with the wakeup call? There is still another **earthquake** to come and all will surely know that **Revelation 9** has truly come to light.

Bypass your mind church and walk with Me in complete and total obedience to what I have called you forth to do. Repent and follow Me saith the Father, for I will truly lead you by the still waters in this age of great tribulation.

> **Revelation 9 (NIV)**
> The fifth angel sounded his trumpet, and I saw a star that had fallen from the sky to the earth. The star was given the key to the shaft of the Abyss. When he opened the Abyss, smoke rose from it like the smoke from a gigantic furnace. The sun and sky were darkened by the smoke from the Abyss. And out of the smoke locusts came down on the earth and were given power like that of scorpions of the earth. They were told not to harm the grass of the earth or any plant or tree, but only those people who did not have the seal of God on their foreheads. They were not allowed to kill them but only to torture them for five months. And the agony they suffered was like that of the sting of a scorpion when it strikes. During those days people will seek death but will not find it; they will long to die, but death will elude them.
>
> The locusts looked like horses prepared for battle. On their heads they wore something like crowns of gold, and their faces resembled human faces. Their hair was like women's hair, and their teeth were like lions' teeth. They had

breastplates like breastplates of iron, and the sound of their wings was like the thundering of many horses and chariots rushing into battle. They had tails with stingers, like scorpions, and in their tails they had power to torment people for five months. They had as king over them the angel of the Abyss, whose name in Hebrew is Abaddon and in Greek is Apollyon (that is, Destroyer).

The first woe is past; two other woes are yet to come. The sixth angel sounded his trumpet, and I heard a voice coming from the four horns of the golden altar that is before God. It said to the sixth angel who had the trumpet, "Release the four angels who are bound at the great river Euphrates." And the four angels who had been kept ready for this very hour and day and month and year were released to kill a third of mankind. The number of the mounted troops was twice ten thousand times ten thousand. I heard their number.

The horses and riders I saw in my vision looked like this: Their breastplates were fiery red, dark blue, and yellow as sulfur. The heads of the horses resembled the heads of lions, and out of their mouths came fire, smoke and sulfur. A third of mankind was killed by the three plagues of fire, smoke and sulfur that came out of their mouths. The power of the horses was in their mouths and in their tails; for their tails were like snakes, having heads with which they inflict injury.

The rest of mankind who were not killed by these plagues still did not repent of the work of their hands; they did not stop worshiping demons, and idols of gold, silver, bronze, stone and wood—idols that cannot see or hear or walk. Nor did they repent of their murders, their magic arts, their sexual immorality or their thefts.

Worst Devastation in American History *(Also in Section III)*

America is about to face the worst devastation in American history. America will undergo what some cities in my word underwent. America is about to see My great wrath poured out on her like never before. Daughter glean from what has already happened and prepare yourself for the oncoming onslaught of great destruction.

You talk about **earthquakes**! America has never seen such an earthquake before. It will disrupt all activities all across the land. Borders will be removed and new boundaries will spring up over night. The onslaught is going to be so great that the world will feel like it is in a tailspin and they will not know how to get out of the tailspin.

It is going to take my true believing churches to bring the world full circle around. They will fall upon their knees, but it will be because of the devastation. This whoremongering nation has brought great fire to my nostrils and I am about ready to blow my nose and burn up all this chaff that is a stench to my nostrils.

(Section III) AMERICA...

No one Wants to Save the Lost in America

My daughter, this is the last millennium before the return of My Son. Much must be accomplished in a very short period of time.

I must have those who will surrender their all and all unto Me. I must have their eyes, ears, and mouth. They must go forth in My might and in My Power conquering on all sides.

Even now, little one, the earth is travailing to give birth to My Holy Spirit movement. The time for birth has been set and no one can stop the clock this time, for all things must occur on time.

Great multitudes are standing in the valley of decision in **America** and there is no preacher to send to the multitudes. All want to go overseas, but no one wants to save the lost in **America.**

America, the land of the free and proud. Oh, My **America**, how I weep over you just as I did over Jerusalem. Jerusalem would not heed My voice either. Circumstances are occurring to cause the supernatural to take place in My Body. All who will surrender and come forth at this given time shall be filled with My supernatural powers.

Time is running out and there is so much to accomplish. I am searching the hearts of all men, to find the ones that will remain faithful and true in the midst of the hottest battles hell has to throw at My church. My church shall come out victorious. I have spoken and so shall it be.

I have promised and I am bringing My promises to pass. You just stand back and watch My salvation at work on all sides.

Know that I am the God of Abraham, Isaac and Jacob and I am the God of this church age also.

WHERE ARE MY CHILDREN?

Where are My Children? Where are they? I have given instruction after instruction to prepare for the days ahead, but My children are not heeding the call. I have spoken of the devastation that is coming upon the land, but very few are listening. Where are My children? Their heads are stuck in the sand, believing the false prophets of this land that are telling them that they are safe and I would not allow harm to come to **America**. My Children, where are you? You are not listening! You are not heeding the sound of the trumpet! You are being deceived! Where are you?

Many are the afflictions of the righteous, but I do deliver them out of them all. You have nothing to fear, as long as you draw close to Me and abide under the shadow of the Almighty. Yes, the devastation is coming, but I will keep Mine safe. I will not allow the storm to destroy those that are mine. Many are still trusting in their false gods. Many are still looking to man to provide. But I say unto you, it is only I that can provide true safety. It is only I that can provide fresh manna from heaven. Did I not feed the multitude more than once in My Word with a few fishes and loaves? Can I not do the same today? Or am I a God whose arm is too short?

Come My little ones, don't you see the snare of the enemy at your feet? Don't you see the <u>false witnesses</u> that have come upon this land? Come My little ones Come to the full knowledge that the enemy has sent forth a lie and My children are believing the lie and not the truth of My Word. <u>Nobody can explain away My Word</u>, no matter how hard they try. Absolutely nobody!

Where were you when I formed the heavens and the earth? You were a void at that given time. But I was there. I formed the heavens and the earth. I breathed My breathe into every living thing. Oh what fools My children have become. They look around them and proclaim victory, when there is no victory, **because they have <u>not</u> kicked the enemy out of their camps**. Do not be deceived little ones; I truly will not be mocked. I am still sitting on My throne in My throne room and I am still ruling and reigning over this earth. What I <u>have</u> spoken will come to pass. What I <u>speak</u> will come to pass. All other things are sinking sand, but My Word is truth and it is light to those who find it.

Come little ones, come unto Me those who are heavy laden and I will surely give you rest. Come and allow Me to carry your heavy burdens. Come I say, Come unto Me and find <u>absolute</u> security in My Everlasting Arms of Protection.

Come even this hour, for the hour is late and the darkness is becoming darker and soon there will be no opportunity to come through the open door, for the door is already being shut. The age of the gentiles is closing and I am opening up the door of opportunity for the lost to now come into My Kingdom authority. Come Church! Come into the fullness of who I am.

Job 38:4 (TLB)
"Where were you when I laid the foundations of the earth? Tell me, if you know so much.

Psalm 34:19 (TLB)
The good man does not escape all troubles—he has them

too. But the Lord helps him in each and every one.

Matthew 14:16-21 (TLB)
But Jesus replied, "That isn't necessary—you feed them!" "What!" they exclaimed. "We have exactly five small loaves of bread and two fish!" "Bring them here," he said.

Then he told the people to sit down on the grass; and he took the five loaves and two fish, looked up into the sky, and asked God's blessing on the meal, then broke the loaves apart and gave them to the disciples to place before the people. And everyone ate until full! And when the scraps were picked up afterwards, there were twelve basketfuls left over! (About five thousand men were in the crowd that day, besides all the women and children.)

Matthew 15:33-38 (TLB)
The disciples replied, "And where would we get enough here in the desert for all this mob to eat?" Jesus asked them, "How much food do you have?" And they replied, "Seven loaves of bread and a few small fish!"

Then Jesus told all of the people to sit down on the ground, and he took the seven loaves and the fish, and gave thanks to God for them, and divided them into pieces, and gave them to the disciples who presented them to the crowd and everyone ate until full—four thousand men besides the women and children! And afterwards, when the scraps were picked up, there were seven basketfuls left over!

Matthew 16:9-10 (TLB)
Won't you ever understand? Don't you remember at all the five thousand I fed with five loaves, and the basketfuls left over? Don't you remember the four thousand I fed, and all that was left?

Psalm 27:12 (TLB)
Don't let them get me, Lord! Don't let me fall into their hands! For they accuse me of things I never did, and all the while are plotting cruelty.

Matthew 11:28 (TLB)
Come to me and I will give you rest—all of you who work so hard beneath a heavy yoke. Wear my yoke—for it fits perfectly—and let me teach you; for I am gentle and humble,

and you shall find rest for your souls; for I give you only light burdens."

John 12:35 (TLB)
Jesus replied, "My light will shine out for you just a little while longer. Walk in it while you can, and go where you want to go before the darkness falls, for then it will be too late for you to find your way."

Psalm 91:1 (TLB)
We live within the shadow of the Almighty, sheltered by the God who is above all gods.

Revival to Sweep Across America

God gave me **Jeremiah 12**

Jeremiah 12 (TLB)
O Lord, you always give me justice when I bring a case before you to decide. Now let me bring you this complaint: Why are the wicked so prosperous? Why are evil men so happy? You plant them. They take root and their business grows. Their profits multiply, and they are rich. They say, "Thank God!" But in their hearts they give no credit to you. But as for me—Lord, you know my heart—you know how much it longs for you. (And I am poor, O Lord!) Lord, drag them off like helpless sheep to the slaughter. Judge them, O God!

How long must this land of yours put up with all their goings-on? Even the grass of the field groans and weeps over their wicked deeds! The wild animals and birds have moved away, leaving the land deserted. Yet the people say, "God won't bring judgment on us. We're perfectly safe!"

The Lord replied to me: If racing with mere men—these men of Anathoth—has wearied you, how will you race against horses, against the king, his court, and all his evil priests? If you stumble and fall on open ground, what will you do in Jordan's jungles? Even your own brothers, your own family, have turned against you. They have plotted to call for a mob to lynch you. Don't trust them, no matter how pleasantly they speak. Don't believe them.

Then the Lord said: I have abandoned my people, my inheritance; I have surrendered my dearest ones to their enemies. My people have roared at me like a lion of the forest, so I have treated them as though I hated them. My people have fallen. I will bring upon them swarms of vultures and wild animals to pick the flesh from their corpses.

Many foreign rulers have ravaged my vineyard, trampling down the vines, and turning all its beauty into barren wilderness. They have made it desolate; I hear its mournful cry. The whole land is desolate and no one cares. Destroying armies plunder the land; the sword of the Lord devours from one end of the nation to the other; nothing shall escape. My people have sown wheat but reaped thorns; they have worked hard, but it does them no good. They shall harvest a crop of shame, for the fierce anger of the Lord is upon them.

And now the Lord says this to the evil nations, the nations surrounding the land God gave his people Israel: See, I will force you from your land just as Judah will be forced from hers; but afterwards I will return and have compassion on all of you and will bring you home to your own land again, each man to his inheritance. And if these heathen nations quickly learn my people's ways and claim me as their God instead of Baal (whom they taught my people to worship), then they shall be strong among my people. But any nation refusing to obey me will be expelled again and finished, says the Lord.

This revival is so different.

This revival is bringing the sin to the surface and dealing with it once and for all. This is a revival of complete repentance; never to go back to the sin nature ever again. Lay at My feet continually and then watch Me move on your behalf. This revival will bring nations to its knees. It will show forth the goodness of the Father. The last revival brought Holy laughter, but it did not have a long lasting effect. The last revival was one of GREAT joy, but not GREAT salvation. I am on the move and I have brought revival to this land. All must step into this revival of salvation in order to receive anything out of it. If you do not let go of your sins, you will be forever lost, for this is the last great revival to sweep across America before the coming of My son for the second time.

America Will no Longer be America

It is time to get the house in order. It is time that everything unclean is eliminated. For the evil in this world is increasing and the evil will overtake the good in some areas. There is much being said about 911 and how terrible it was, but what is coming upon **America** is far more outreaching than 911. Many will truly run to and fro and many will take their lives at this given time. Many will not be able to distinguish the good from the evil, for their minds will have been darkened by the hardening of their hearts. There will be much tribulation at this given time. Woe upon woe will increase across this great **America**. Yes, some have repented and that is good, but so many more have not and that is what has brought this judgment upon My Chosen Land **America**. I had set America apart as a sign and a wonder of My Great Love for My people. But now it is being set apart to demonstrate My Great Wrath for a people that would not turn to the living Father, but chose to serve their own Baals.

America will no longer be **America** as you all have known her. She will be distorted on all sides and she will lack in every area. But the bright side is, this move of mine will bring a landslide salvation to **America**. Sodom and Gomorrah have nothing on **America**. She has reached down into the bowels of hell and pulled every abomination to the surface and she has played the harlot over and over again. NOW! Now, I will have My say so. The saints that have gone before are crying out for revenge on this perverted land, and I am answering their cries.

When will they repent? You just watch, saith the Father! You just watch!

Oh America...

There is a movement abroad that wants to bring devastation to this United Sates of **America**, the land that I so love. My peoples must fast and pray as never before, for the movement is surely set afoot even as we speak. The darkness, even the gross darkness that I have spoken of is creeping across **America**. Many homes and lives will be lost during this season of Great Darkness.

Oh America, Why did you **not** want My Mercy?

Why did you want a King?

I would have given you all that you wanted, but you rejected Me for the king. Now, there is nothing else that I can do, but bring My wrath. The bowls of judgment will now come forward and all will know that it is the handy work of the almighty one.

America, why would you **not** dispose of your idols?

Why would you **not** turn from your wicked evil ways and repent?

Why do you want to slaughter My precious babies?

Why do you want to desecrate My Holy Marriage vows?

Why **America** Why?

You have set the course of judgment upon your own selves and there is nothing I can do. My hand will **not** be stayed. You who are called by My name, apply the blood line over your families, churches and towns. For the death angel has been set forth, even as we speak.

Oh, it could have been so different. I sent My prophets to warn you, but you would not heed those warnings. Now what? You are asking. You think your King can pull this off! I say nay! For I am the only true King and God, even though you have chosen your own fleshly King and God. You will now find out what your choice will do for you.

Churches/Pastors, where were you? Why did you not call a solemn assembly? Why did you not stand between the porch and the altar and cry out to the Living God, instead of your Mickey Mouse idols? Why, Why, Why?

I am truly weeping over you **America.** My tears run hot down My face this day. I gave you space to repent and you would not. You think it is going to become easier? I beg to differ with you. You have seen nothing yet. Hard times are coming upon the economy and because they come upon the economy, they will affect every other aspect of your life. Rachel, cry out for your children, for your children will go to war with each other and many lives are going to be lost.

Awake **America.** Awake out of your slumber and cry out to the one true and living God. Awake! I say Awake from your slumber.

I am so deeply saddened. My heart is broken. I warned what you were about to do, but you turned your foolish head away from Me and you looked to your idol. Well, you have your idol and now let's see what your idol will do for you.

Gloom and Despair await all who voted in the idol. Those who voted in the idol were not mine, for Mine elect sought My face and they heard My voice and they cried out for Mercy; and those I am now covering with the precious blood of My Son and it is those that I will keep in this horrible day of wrath that is coming upon you **America.**

Do I still love you? Absolutely, but you have become a spoiled nation. One with no restraints and now you must feel My chastening Rod upon your backs.

Woe! Woe! Woe! Sorrow upon sorrow! You are getting what you asked for!

Much Calamity is Coming upon America

Much calamity is coming upon **America.** Much-much calamity is coming and hearts will fail because of fear. Many will run to and fro and they will faint with fear. They have no understanding of this end time event. They have been wondering around in a daze and the truth is not revealed to My people. Therefore the enemy has them for fair game. I warned and I warned, but not all heeded My warnings and now the days of calamity have come upon **America.** You shall see war on the shores of **America.** You shall see much blood shed on the shores of **America.** It will seem like the enemy is triumphing over My people, but if My people will run into the hedge of refuge, I will protect them from all harm. I will provide the way of escape. For this is the hour that I have spoken of in Joel. My Glory shall fall over this land and it shall cover My peoples and a great harvest of souls will be seen throughout the United States of **America.** Be prepared little one. Be prepared for the great influx of lost and dying souls.

America has not learned to bow her knee to the Living Saviour and therefore she must suffer under the hand of the Almighty One. I love My Country and therefore I must chastise her and bring her to her knees before the enemy totally destroys her.

Be prepared little one. Be prepared.

Destruction is Coming Upon America

Many souls are being weighed in the balance even as we speak and many more are sliding into the great abyss every second of every day. Warn My people to be prepared for the great and terrible day of the second coming of My Son. I say great, because it will be a wonderful, marvelous day for those who have made themselves ready. But it will be terrible for those who have not prepared themselves and who make their bed in sheol. Daughter, it is no laughing matter. It is real! It is serious! My Son is coming the second time and then the great white throne judgment will occur. Daughter, warn My people at every turn. Tell them to turn from their wicked evil ways. The destruction is coming upon **America** and only those who are standing in My Shekinah presence will be sustained through this terrible day of tribulations.

> **Revelation 20:11-15 (NKJV)**
> Then I saw a great white throne and Him who sat on it, from whose face the earth and the heaven fled away. And there was found no place for them. And I saw the dead, small and great, standing beforeGod, and books were opened. And another book was opened, which is the Book of Life. And the dead were judged according to their works, by the things which were written in the books. The sea gave up the dead who were in it, and Death and Hades delivered up the dead who were in them. And they were judged, each one according to his works. Then Death and Hades were cast into the lake of fire. This is the second death. And anyone not found written in the Book of Life was cast into the lake of fire.
>
> **Daniel 5:27 (NKJV)**
> TEKEL: You have been weighed in the balances, and found wanting;
>
> **Isaiah 5:14 (NKJV)**
> Therefore Sheol has enlarged itself
> And opened its mouth beyond measure;

Their glory and their multitude and their pomp,
And he who is jubilant, shall descend into it.

Isaiah 14:11 (NKJV)
Your pomp is brought down to Sheol,
And the sound of your stringed instruments;
The maggot is spread under you,
And worms cover you.'

Saints of God, prepare yourselves for the second coming of Jesus Christ. Seek His face at every turn and make yourselves ready.

Enemy Upon American Soil

The Countdown to Armageddon has begun. There will not only be wars and rumors of wars, but also there will be outbreaks of war all over (this) land. You will soon see the enemy come upon **American** soil. The last trump has been blown and all out war has begun. Nation against nation! Peoples against peoples! All over this land bloodshed. Disaster after disaster. BUT in the midst of it all I will show My Glory through out this land. You are right on, My people need to be NOW people, because I am not in the future and I am not in the past. I am in the (RIGHT NOW) time of My timetable.

Be prepared for one of the biggest onslaughts of the enemy against the church that has ever occurred. The enemy is raging and he will stop at nothing to bring My churches down to total destruction. But know in your heart of hearts that I am now and always will be in full and total control of all things.

Take up the sword and advance. Do not stand still and allow the enemy to plow you over church, but advance forward and I will be with you, just as I was with Joshua.

Full blast church, go forward full blast, no holds barred. This is the time of the greatest conquest for the church, even though the enemy he does rage.

Then two days later Our Father told me to read Lamentations.

I humbly submit this to you, it is not to frighten the people, but to warn them of what is to come.

God has spoken to me and said the watchmen must be on the wall to hear his voice for the people.

America bow Your Knee

Take pen in hand and write, for I am about to reveal to this nation what is coming upon this nation in greater wrath than ever seen before.

Do you not see that this Nation will not repent? Take a good look at New Orleans. What is this Nation doing? They are restoring on sin. They are **not** restoring on My foundation.

Woe upon woe for this Nation. I have spoken and so shall it be.

America! America! America when will you look to the Author and Finisher of your lives? When will you take Me at My Word and obey My voice? When?

As My Son wept over Jerusalem, I am weeping over this great nation that I had set apart for My good pleasure and to show the others what I do for those who find favor in My eyes.

America what have you done? What have you done? You are full of harlotry's and you worship other idols. I have spoken from My word and said: there shall be no other idols before Me.

Why won't you take a look at My word and believe what I say?

I placed many parables in My word about disobedience and also obedience, but you pay no heed to what I have said.

America, where are you at? What is the problem here? I know you have sold yourself into slavery to the enemy, but I came and made the way of escape so many times, but you will not take that way of escape. Are you so blinded that you cannot really see the fruitlessness of your works?

Bow your knee **America!** Bow your knee once and for all. For I have spoken and so shall it be.

Come into My secret pavilion of safety and be shielded from the evil one.

Judgment Upon America

The nations as you know them will soon change. There is much disaster coming to the nations of **America**. I have spoken words of encouragement over the nations. I have spoken words of warning over the nations. But the nations continue to go their own ways. They have no heart for Me, the true and living God. They continue down the path of pure destruction.

You shall surely see Phoenix fall. You shall also see much destruction come to Florida. The websites will soon be overflowing with the destructions that will be going on around them. There will be many cries for help, but to no avail.

This is a very integral time for the nations. My prophets are being shunned. My Evangelists are being shunned. My Holy Spirit filled Ministers are being shunned! But all that is coming to an end and you shall see all three of these being looked upon with much respect and they will be called upon to speak what thus saith the Lord, for the nations will need to hear from the Living God at this given time.

Many will fall; and many will rise to great prominence. For this is the hour that was spoken of by My prophet Joel. You shall surely see great signs and wonders both upon the earth and coming out of the heavenly realm.

You have been speaking about the catastrophes --- fires --- that are going on, and you have been saying I know that this is the hand of judgment on **America,** and you are right on little one, you are right on. But do you understand that even with all this, I have not gotten **America's** attention?

America is on a downward spiral of destruction, and they do not even understand what is going on around about them. They are judging and pointing the finger and all the while, they need to look upon their selves and their wicked evil ways. For it is the wickedness, in each heart, that is causing this great judgment to fall upon America.

The nations will surely tremble and the earth shall surely shake, but I have stayed My hand of judgment as long as I intend to, and nothing can stop Me now.

The prayers at this given time should be; **Your will be done, Oh Lord!**

Daughter, each home must raise up a standard of Holiness and Peace and remain under that standard at all cost. For it is only the Holy that shall survive the attacks that are coming upon this land, even as we speak.

Will Phoenix cause others to turn? **Not so**, but they shall see total destruction on every side because of their stubbornness to yield to My voice and My signs to the Nations. Only those who are walking in complete Holiness will survive at this given hour -- all others will be slain by the sword.

Judgment Upon My Beloved America

Tell My people that it is too late to turn back the hands of time. The warring angels have been sent forth to do My bidding.

This is the hour spoken of in **Joel chapter 2**. This is the hour when the whole world will sway under My mighty hand of judgment.

Sodom and Gomorrah would have repented by now, but not **America,** My beloved **America.** She is so caught up in her idol worship, that she will not abide by My voice any longer. So I must bring My heavy hand of judgment down upon her.

You will see a great separation occur in My churches at this given time, for I have truly sent the reapers forth to gather in the harvest.

Solomon's temple will be rebuilt and all will see the miracle working power of a Mighty God at work at this given time.

Who is there that can stand before Me? No one!

All those that have spoken against Me and said they would consume Me, will now be consumed. They are about to see what power and authority that I have.

My Kingdom Come, My Will Be Done, On Earth As It Is In Heaven!

Joel 2 (MSG)
Blow the ram's horn trumpet in Zion!
   Trumpet the alarm on my holy mountain!
Shake the country up!
   God's Judgment's on its way—the Day's almost here!
A black day! A Doomsday!
   Clouds with no silver lining!
Like dawn light moving over the mountains,
   a huge army is coming.
There's never been anything like it

and never will be again.
Wildfire burns everything before this army
    and fire licks up everything in its wake.
Before it arrives, the country is like the Garden of Eden.
    When it leaves, it is Death Valley.
    Nothing escapes unscathed.

The locust army seems all horses—
    galloping horses, an army of horses.
It sounds like thunder
    leaping on mountain ridges,
Or like the roar of wildfire
    through grass and brush,
Or like an invincible army shouting for blood,
    ready to fight, straining at the bit.
At the sight of this army,
    the people panic, faces white with terror.

The invaders charge.
    They climb barricades. Nothing stops them.
Each soldier does what he's told,
    so disciplined, so determined.
They don't get in each other's way.
    Each one knows his job and does it.
Undaunted and fearless,
    unswerving, unstoppable.
They storm the city,
    swarm its defenses,
Loot the houses,
    breaking down doors, smashing windows.
They arrive like an earthquake,
    sweep through like a tornado.
Sun and moon turn out their lights,
    stars black out.
God himself bellows in thunder
    as he commands his forces.
Look at the size of that army!
    And the strength of those who obey him!
God's Judgment Day—great and terrible.
    Who can possibly survive this?

But there's also this, it's not too late—
    God's personal Message!—
"Come back to me and really mean it!

End Time Prophecies

Come fasting and weeping, sorry for your sins!"

Change your life, not just your clothes.
  Come back to God, your God.
And here's why: God is kind and merciful.
  He takes a deep breath, puts up with a lot,
This most patient God, extravagant in love,
  always ready to cancel catastrophe.
Who knows? Maybe he'll do it now,
  maybe he'll turn around and show pity.
Maybe, when all's said and done,
  there'll be blessings full and robust for your God!

Blow the ram's horn trumpet in Zion!
  Declare a day of repentance, a holy fast day.
Call a public meeting.
  Get everyone there. Consecrate the congregation.
Make sure the elders come,
  but bring in the children, too, even the nursing babies,
Even men and women on their honeymoon—
  interrupt them and get them there.
Between Sanctuary entrance and altar,
  let the priests, God's servants, weep tears of repentance.
Let them intercede: "Have mercy, God, on your people!
  Don't abandon your heritage to contempt.
Don't let the pagans take over and rule them
  and sneer, 'And so where is this God of theirs?'"

At that, God went into action to get his land back.
  He took pity on his people.
God answered and spoke to his people,
  "Look, listen—I'm sending a gift:
Grain and wine and olive oil.
  The fast is over—eat your fill!
I won't expose you any longer
  to contempt among the pagans.
I'll head off the final enemy coming out of the north
  and dump them in a wasteland.
Half of them will end up in the Dead Sea,
  the other half in the Mediterranean.
There they'll rot, a stench to high heaven.
  The bigger the enemy, the stronger the stench!"

Fear not, Earth! Be glad and celebrate!

God has done great things.
Fear not, wild animals!
   The fields and meadows are greening up.
The trees are bearing fruit again:
   a bumper crop of fig trees and vines!
Children of Zion, celebrate!
   Be glad in your God.
He's giving you a teacher
   to train you how to live right—
Teaching, like rain out of heaven, showers of words
   to refresh and nourish your soul, just as he used to do.
And plenty of food for your body—silos full of grain,
   casks of wine and barrels of olive oil.

"I'll make up for the years of the locust,
   the great locust devastation—
Locusts savage, locusts deadly,
   fierce locusts, locusts of doom,
That great locust invasion
   I sent your way.
You'll eat your fill of good food.
   You'll be full of praises to your God,
The God who has set you back on your heels in wonder.
   Never again will my people be despised.
You'll know without question
   that I'm in the thick of life with Israel,
That I'm your God, yes, your God,
   the one and only real God.
Never again will my people be despised.

"And that's just the beginning: After that—
"I will pour out my Spirit
   on every kind of people:
Your sons will prophesy,
   also your daughters.
Your old men will dream,
   your young men will see visions.
I'll even pour out my Spirit on the servants,
   men and women both.
I'll set wonders in the sky above
   and signs on the earth below:
Blood and fire and billowing smoke,
   the sun turning black and the moon blood-red,
Before the Judgment Day of God,

>   the Day tremendous and awesome.
> Whoever calls, 'Help, God!'
>   gets help.
> On Mount Zion and in Jerusalem
>   there will be a great rescue—just as God said.
> Included in the survivors
>   are those that God calls."

Terror Will Strike America

Terror is going to strike **America** in an unprecedented way. I am about to unleash the hordes of hell on **America**. I have come to set the captives free and this is the only way possible to accomplish what I must accomplish in a short season.

In this short season, I am opening up a window of opportunity for My people to walk into the blessings of Abraham, Isaac and Jacob. If they will walk through this window of opportunity, they will find their finances unleashed and will walk in financial freedom. Some will not, and they will stay in financial bondage.

I am about My business and I am not playing games. This is the time of great salvations amongst the land. This is the opportunity of a lifetime in My church age. This is the greater works time. (If) My Body will rise up and walk in it.

Who is to say that I am not God? Who is it to say that I cannot conquer the enemy on every side? Who is it that sits idly by and watches the souls going to Hell every second of every day?

It is a church that is in a deep state of lethargy. At this given time I am pulling the church out of this state of deep lethargy. Some will answer the call and others will stay in their state of slumber. But all that will arise out of lethargy at this given time will be blessed without measure and they shall surely see the great signs, wonders and miracles unleashed in their ministries.

Go forth church! Go forth unhindered! Go forth unconquered! But go forth!

Heavy Hand of Judgment

What I tell you today will resound around the world. I am coming after My bride and My bride is not ready. I have wooed and I have wooed but to no avail.

This time I am coming with My Sword and I am going to cut off and I am going to separate the wheat from the chaff in My House. I am the Father of all wrath at this given time, for **America** will not repent of her wicked evil ways and it has become an abomination unto Me, the True and Living God. It is ok, for now they will receive exactly what they have been crying out for. They will have their other God and then they will see the error of their ways, but it is now to late, for I will not relent this time. My arm is not so short that I could not have reached down and pulled **America** out of her pig sty, but she continues on unrelenting of her vile evil ways and I am disgusted with this whole mess that lies before Me.

The whole earth will sway under My Heavy Hand of Judgment and all shall know that I am God of all creation. It will now be time for the great harvest to be brought in. It is now time for My Mighty Miracles. Just stand back and be silent for you shall surely see the salvation of the Lord at hand at this given time.

Woe Upon Woe Upon This Land

The winds of adversity have begun to blow across this **land** and even at this given hour much destruction is upon this **land.**

This is the time of great harvest. Harvest of souls and a harvest of reaping what has been sown.

How many will suffer at the hands of a merciful Father, but will not prevail?

How many will suffer at the hands of a merciful Father and will understand that I am working all things out for the good of those who love Me?

As you stand back and watch, you shall see who is really faithful and who is pretending to be My children.

Many ships will sink in this season of warfare. Many will not be able to rightly divide what is going on in the spirit realm and they will walk circumspectly to My Word.

Take control of your atmosphere church. Take control and be able to withstand the winds of adversity that have already begun to blow across this land.

How the mighty have fallen. You shall surely see the mighty ones fall under My Sword of chastisement.

I am coming after My bride. Is My bride ready? Or are you like the five foolish virgins?

Woe upon woe is now upon this land.

Take My Grace and Mercy and abide under the shadow of the almighty and do not allow the enemy any inroads into your lives. For this is the time of great deception.

Deception will cover the land as never before. Deception has also crept into My houses, but I am going to uncover all forms of deception, and only the truth will prevail in this given hour of total devastation upon this land.

America – Judgment - My Great Wrath

It is time to get the house in order. It is time that everything unclean is eliminated. For the evil in this world is increasing and the evil will overtake the good in some areas.

There is much being said about 9-11 and how terrible it was, but what is coming upon **America** is far more outreaching than 9-11.

Many will truly run to and fro and many will take their lives at this given time. Many will not be able to distinguish the good from the evil, for their minds will have been darkened by the hardening of their hearts. There will be much tribulation at this given time.

Woe upon woe will increase across this great **America**

Yes, some have repented and that is good, but so many more have not and that is what has brought this judgment upon My Chosen Land **America.**

I had set **America** apart as a sign and a wonder of My Great Love for My people. But now it is being set apart to demonstrate My Great Wrath for a people that would not turn to the living Father, but chose to serve their own Baals.

America will no longer be **America** as you all have known her. She will be distorted on all sides and she will lack in every area. But the bright side is, this move of mine will bring a landslide salvation to **America.**

Sodom and Gomorrah have nothing on **America.** She has reached down into the bowels of hell and pulled every abomination to the surface and she has played the harlot over and over again.

NOW! Now, I will have My say so. The saints that have gone before are crying out for revenge on this perverted land, and I am answering their cries.

When will they repent? You just watch, saith the Father! You just watch!

I will repay saith the Lord, I will repay evil for evil. And good for good in this end time judgment.

Getting America's Undivided Attention

America is about to be invaded on all sides. The likes of which no one has ever seen. War will be brought right into your own back yards. Sin has prevailed, even though I have asked for repentance.

I will have a purified church. I will have a purified land. I always do whatever it takes to get My people's attention.

Now is no different than in the past. Many out there playing the harlot, when I have called them to sanctify themselves a holy people, ones without spot nor wrinkle.

You just watch what I am about to do. You just stand back and see the salvation of the Lord on all sides, for truly I am coming after **America** and I will get her undivided attention.

Great Explosion -Not End Until it is Finished

There will be a great explosion that will be heard across this land. Much destruction is still on the way.

When will it all end, they ask? It will end when it is finished and not until then. I am going to do a complete works in **America** and all shall surely know that I am in full and complete control of all things.

Sorrow is About to Sweep Across This Nation

My beloved one. Much sorrow is about to be swept across this nation that you know as **America.** Many will be running to and fro and many will lose their lives at this given time. I am standing before you this day as a true and living Father. I have set My plans in motion and they will not be stopped. There is a plan that has been set before the beginning of the foundations of this earth and I am implementing it at this given time.

Much will happen in a few short weeks that will change this world forever. I love you and all My people, but too much has been done and too much has been said that did not edify or lift Me up.

Where will it all end, is what so many are asking Me at this given time. It will end in one of the biggest revivals this world has ever seen. It will end with My people truly serving Me as a true and living Father.

My churches will be filled to overflowing and My name will be preached in every pulpit. No more self-exaltation. No more moneychangers in My house. I will supply the needs. I have always taken care of My own and I shall always take care of My own.

Great Revival

The Fullness of Time has come upon My church. It is time for revival to strike across this great **land.** Amidst the great destruction that is going on, I am now pouring out My Spirit upon all flesh. All flesh will know and see the fullness of their God. Whether it be Me, or the enemy they shall know the fullness of their God.

Do not be afraid of what you hear Me say to the people. It is time for them to understand their days of fulfillment. They worked hard for this day and they need to know what their labors have brought them. Some have labored for the Kingdom of God and some have labored to their own destruction. I once told you (many times) that this day was coming and there would be great gnashing of teeth.

Do not be afraid of the people's faces any longer. Let them say and do what they have already pre-purposed in their heart to do. This is the long awaited day for many. They have been wondering where it is all going to end and now they shall know.

The destruction that lies around about and will still come is of little importance now. I have shifted in the heavenlies and I am now working on one of the greatest revivals this world has ever seen. Many are going to miss out in this revival. Many others are going to see their ministries blossom as never before.

I truly do speak in parables, for My people are still not ready to hear the truth of My Word, but all that is shifting also. You shall see this great shifting occur right before your very eyes. Suddenly in an instant I will bring to pass all the promises.

Just as I took My disciples aside with Me and told them the truth of things to come, I have been taking My true disciples aside and sharing the truth of the end times. Just like Paul, I have set them apart and shared many heavenly things with them and now they shall share in the rewards just as My disciples in My Word did.

Many new songs will be written in the days ahead. For I am putting a new song in the hearts of My disciples and they shall sing these new songs for Me Church stay humble before a humble King and allow Me (always) to lead, guide, and direct your every word and your every footstep. You have been awaiting this day for quite some time now. The riches of heaven are being poured out and you shall know the Fullness of Time.

Galatians 4: 3-4 (NKJV)
Even so we, when we were children, were in bondage under

the elements of the world. But when the fullness of the time had come, God sent forth His Son, born of a woman, born under the law,

Ephesians 1: 7-12 (NKJV)
In Him we have redemption through His blood, the forgiveness of sins, according to the riches of His grace which He made to abound toward us in all wisdom and prudence, having made known to us the mystery of His will, according to His good pleasure which He purposed in Himself, that in the dispensation of the fullness of the times He might gather together in one all things in Christ, both which are in heaven and which are on earth—in Him. In Him also we have obtained an inheritance, being predestined according to the purpose of Him who works all things according to the counsel of His will, that we who first trusted in Christ should be to the praise of His glory.

Delaware Revival

Much destruction little one, much destruction is coming upon this **land.** There will be many heartaches and many tears, but this must happen. This must occur, for I have no other choice. My people who are called by My name have blasphemed my name for the last time. NOW, right now is the time for salvation, but they are refusing the salvation call. I am sorry for the disaster that is coming, but I have no other choice.

My little one, do not get in the line of fire. Stay clear at all cost. The enemy will try to pull you into the destruction that is about to come, but do not get caught in the crossfire. I have asked you to stand still and watch the salvation of the Lord and I am still giving you the same mandate. It is finished! It is finished! I have no other recourse, but destruction upon the land.

My callings are sure, they are yes and amen, but all else will perish. The roadblocks have been set in place and many will perish at this given time. It will be an ugly monster that seems out of control, but I truly am in control of this devastation.

Daughter, you cannot change the course of events that must take place. You have cried out to Me and cried out to Me, and I have worked a works, but they would not heed to the works, therefore devastation must come upon the land.

Delaware will have revival, and the revival fires will spread to other nations.

I have a plan and a purpose for Delaware and it will surely come to pass.

Hold tightly to the horns of the altar, for I am about to give Delaware a great visitation of My Holy Spirit.

America and Marriages

Great destruction! Great destruction all over this earth. Never in the history of man has such destruction been seen. I have spoken and so shall it be.

Land upon land will be affected. I have given space for repentance, but to no avail. Yes there is a remnant that has bowed their knees, but so very few.

As it was in the days of Noah, so it is at this given time. Much wine is being drunk, and they reel about to and fro looking to their little god to bring them pleasure after pleasure. It will not end, so I will bring these destructions that I have and am speaking of.

Woe upon woe will be seen across this great nation. There will be little or no food to partake of. You will see starvation on all fronts. I have now brought My wrath upon **America** shores, but **America** is refusing to believe it is I.

Yes, the good are perishing with the evil, but I have warned. Some say it is not fair. Some say that I am an unjust God. But look at what they have done to the blood of My Son who hung on Calvary's hill for their salvation! They have trampled it under foot over and over again. They say all is fair play, but not so.

Look at My children's marriages. They lie in ruin and shame, because My Body plays the harlot. I have said Woe unto those who would trample under foot the marriages I have placed together, but to no avail.

My Words mean absolutely nothing to My Body they just go on playing the harlot. But soon you will also see the separation that I do on My people's behalf. For I am tired of the game playing and I am coming with a sword to devour all that would not yield to the call of total repentance and restoration to their marriages. This is not a difficult thing that I ask, and those who still play the harlot will suffer the sword.

Many are looking to My People for comfort but they can find none, because My people are walking around in sin and confusion. For sin brings in confusion. And I am going to destroy the confusion in My House and in My marriages. Sin will cease, or My people will be no more. I have spoken and so shall it be. They have blasphemed My Son's name for the last time. Now great judgment and tribulation will overtake My People.

Shake the dust from your feet and move on with Me, saith your Father.

Do not allow the sins of this present world to take you astray, for I am about to destroy the sin nature in My People and then I will bring total destruction to this world, as you know it.

My Son is returning for a spotless bride, one without spot or wrinkle.

Hurry church. Hurry on home with Me and change your

course of worship, before I come and change your course of destiny.

America is Having... A Great Visitation

OK church where are you going from here? The revival that I have spoken of has come. What are you going to do with it? Are you just going to stand and stare, criticize, and rebuke or are you going to jump in the river of living waters and flow with Me?

I have an agenda and it is nothing like your agenda. Many more souls will be healed, set free, delivered from all matter of infirmities. You have seen nothing yet. The outpouring of My Spirit is going to become stronger and stronger and the atmosphere will permeate with My Being.

The great explosion has occurred and it will not stop. Do not linger on the shore line any longer, but jump in head first and partake of My Great Glory. The Glory Cloud will become heavier and heavier. You have seen nothing yet. What I have spoken in Joel is surely coming to pass right before your very eyes.

America is having her last great visitation before the coming of My Son to gather His people on home. The outpouring will usher in the second coming of My Son. Many are fighting over this outpouring. **WHY?**

Can you not believe that I would do this thing? Can you not believe the vessel that I have chosen to work through. My word says, the last shall be first and the first last. What is it to you, whom I use?

If you do what is right, I will surely use you also. Many have been crying out for revival for years now and do you think I will only use one vessel? Who are you kidding? This is not a one man show. I will use many in this great outpouring. Jealousy is running rampant at this given time. Many are in derision over this outpouring. What is really in your heart?

What do you really want out of this whole thing? Come into the overflow and allow Me to use you also. Don't just sit and stare. Don't sit around trying to figure out why I did this the way I did it. Revival fires are being lit all across this nation, and they will ignite wherever there is a handful of faithful believers with pure hearts that want only to see My Glory prevail. It is time to quit all the facades and it is time to become honest with yourselves and repent and allow Me to restore you to your rightful place in My Body.

If you have done wrong, then be big enough to admit it and move on. When your heart was tested, did the vile come forth? Then spew it out and allow Me to heal that part of your being. No man nor no woman can stop this mighty movement. It is here to stay. You can be a part of it or you can allow the enemy to make you bitter and sour and you will miss out on this outpouring of My Glory. I wish to manifest Myself daily all over this planet. Are you ready for your great visitation? That is the true question. Are you ready for your great visitation?

So Much Trauma Hitting America

This is a season of great controversy all over the **land**. My people are truly running to and fro in their minds at this given time trying to figure out what I am doing. There is truly nothing to figure out. It will be plain to see what I am doing in the near future.

So much trauma hitting **America** on all sides. The onslaught of the enemy will grow more intense as the days come forth. He is truly roaring like a lion seeking whom he can devour, but if My church would only realize that he is imitating THE LION OF JUDAH that has come upon the scene, they would not be so restless and they would walk in perfect peace upon My most holy hill and they would be firmly reconciled unto Me at this given time.

Seek not revenge upon your enemies. For they are not your enemies, they are mine and I am preparing a boiling pot for them to fall into. I have spoken much in the days past and I am going to be speaking volumes once again. You will hear My prophets more clearly and with much emphases upon My Spirit. For this is the hour of the Fullness of My Holy Spirit. My Holy Spirit has come upon the scene in all his majesty to lead, guide and direct My chosen generation of born again believers. The path that I have laid out before them is a marvelous path. One with great signs, wonders and miracles. The Supernatural will flow so freely. It will be a time precedented by My Presence on all sides. My church will walk fully in the God Head and they will experience great visitations of My Holy Angels.

A Great Time of Unrest

On the way home from prayer meeting tonight (February 12, 2008) God said: **This United States of America is going to go through a Great Time of Unrest!**

I looked up the meaning of **Unrest: It means: Restlessness; Disquiet; Angry; Discontent; Verging on revolt.**

I truly do believe that this is food for thought. What is **America** really headed for? We have read all the prophecies of the Gross Darkness. We know that what God has placed into motion He will accomplish. He has spoken and told His church when all this comes to the forefront, His true children must be found holding onto the horn's of the altar and to never let go. Question? What are you holding onto?

I Have Come to America

The finality of the times has come upon the land. My Glory is being revealed all across this nation. I will show signs and wonders everywhere in the few short days ahead. There will be not one state untouched. I have spoken and so shall it be.

Control! I am in full and complete control of this new revival of souls that has already begun. I will change every nation, tribe and tongue. There will nothing left untouched by this revival. You shall see manifestations of My Glory all across this nation.

I have come to **America** with this great revival in answer to many prayers that have ascended to the throne room. No weapon formed against this revival shall hinder it. All who will try to take control will lose control of everything. There is absolutely nothing that I will withhold from this revival that is already sweeping the nations. It is line upon line and precept upon precept. It is decent and in order.

Daughter, the church has seen nothing yet. Just you wait and see, this explosion will be heard all across this earth. It will be from Glory to Glory to Glory. Trust Me.

I Keep Warning and Warning *(Also in Section I)*

I am speaking volumes, but still nobody is listening. I keep warning and warning and warning, but nobody cares. They think this all a big hoax that will just disappear.

Daughter, when will they ever learn that this is not going to go away. We are at the end time and the gross darkness is surely covering this earth. The election of this presidency (prophecy given in April 2009) opened up the regions of hell to devour My land. Now, the church must fight as never before. They did not seek My face. They did not adhere to the constitution of the United States of **America** and now they are being sold to foreign countries. Where are the intercessors? Where are those that will lay out before me on behalf of this once great state?

They are too busy trying to keep it together. There is nothing absolutely nothing that is going to keep it together. It is falling apart and it will continue to fall apart. This is what sin will do for a nation. The slaughterer has surely come and he has unleashed all of his fury upon My Great Nation. But then he had to have an open door to work from and this nation gave him a wide door of opportunity.

Stand back My faithful ones. Stand back and do not get caught up in the slaughter of innocent babies. Stand back and pray without ceasing. I will not stay My hand of wrath, but I will save a multitude of souls as you pray without ceasing. It truly is fasting and prayer time for My faith ones. It is surely time that you take up the sword and go forth destroying the enemy at every turn. Do not look around about you. You already know what is occurring. Just fast and pray. Just fast and pray.

I Will Devastate This Whole Earth (Also in Section I)

There are mountains and then there ARE MOUNTAINS! I am calling you forth at this given time to hurdle over the mountain tops and stay securely rooted and grounded in Me.

I know who I am, but My people do not know who they are and the enemy comes again and again to steal from My chosen people.

When will they learn? How long will it take?

For some it will take so long that it will be too late. For others they are going to wise up quickly and they will arise out of the ash heap and serve Me with all of their hearts.

This is the greatest time of decision in the church history. This <u>decision </u>will make or break My church.

It is time to arise up out of the ash heap and serve the Living God and serve Him only, for I will have no other Gods before Me. I am true and I am faithful and I fail not My peoples. Look up peoples!

Look up, for your redemption doth truly draw nigh.

Just as quickly as New Orleans was destroyed, I will devastate this whole earth. Many will be running to and fro. The peoples will be about their normal everyday lives and suddenly out of nowhere I will appear and it will be all over. I have spoken this before and nobody heeded My voice. I am <u>speaking</u> it again and still they will not heed My voice.

Destruction must come upon this **Nation**, for they are making themselves a **Nation** without a Father. They are taking Me out of everything and I am wroth with My peoples.

Come and take counsel from Me, saith the Father. Come and take counsel from Me and learn the truth of what is happening round about you. You are transgressing My laws daily and I will not permit it any longer. You have cast Me asunder. You have brought Me to shame over and over again. Enough is enough and I am tired of this horseplay that you call church and I have come to put an end to it.

Take not counsel from the ungodly, for they are already lost. Seek counsel from Me, for I am your counselor. I and only I have the answers to your questions.

Why do you forsake Me over and over again? Why not just come to the throne of grace and accept all that My Son did for you? WHY? That is My question to you tonight. WHY?

America Will Repent (Also in Section I)

This is My storm and this is My wrath. I have been displeased with this **Nation** for some time now and I have given this nation time to repent, but to no avail. I have run out of time for a lot of things and I must be about My business.

This time of great trouble has been spoken of for years now, but no one would listen. But I will have My way! I will have My way! When all is said and done there will be still many that will not turn to Me, in fact in the midst of these trials there are many who have already turned their back upon Me and cursed Me. They have sold themselves out to the evil one and there is no turning back.

How much more will I do? You just stand back and watch. There is much more to come and I promise you this.

America will repent and they will turn from their wicked evil ways, but not all.

Church upon church will fall at this given time and will not be rebuilt. For I am purging My ministers and all who will not listen and heed My warnings will be taken out of their ministries.

It has been to long now. It has been to long for the sin to rule and reign in My houses.

Watch what I am about to do in My churches. Watch and see that what I have spoken I am doing. Not about to do, but am doing.

This is the time spoken of in Joel chapter 2. Great tribulation! Great tribulation!

Worst Devastation in American History (Also in Section II)

America is about to face the worst devastation in **American** history. **America** will undergo what some cities in my word underwent. **America** is about to see My great wrath poured out on her like never before. Daughter glean from what has already happened and prepare yourself for the oncoming onslaught of great destruction.

You talk about earthquakes! **America** has never seen such an earthquake before. It will disrupt all activities all across the land. Borders will be removed and new boundaries will spring up over night. The onslaught is going to be so great that the world will feel like it is in a tailspin and they will not know how to get out of the tailspin.

It is going to take my true believing churches to bring the world full circle around. They will fall upon their knees, but it will be because of the devastation. This whoremongering nation has brought great fire to my nostrils and I am about ready to blow my nose and burn up all this chaff that is a stench to my nostrils.

Revelation 9 – Earthquake Coming (Also in Section II)

I long for My people who call Me by name to come into the Holy of Holies and worship with Me there. I long for them to come into the place of everlasting Love and Safety. But they will not. They continue to hang around the cesspools of Sodom and Gomorrah and they no longer abide under the shadow of the Almighty, but they continue to go down their own path of destruction.

I am worthy to be praised and I am demanding praise from My people at this given time. All shall see the salvation of the Lord, but to what degree? Will they truly walk in salvation, or will they stand idly by and watch as others go on with Me and they are consumed with the cares and idols of this world?

Only time will tell, and time will surely tell, saith the Father, for I am going to bring it all out into the light. Every dot and every tittle. And all will see that I am God and that I have not forsaken My own. I have shown My hand of wrath, but still My church, the ones that call Me by My name, is still going their own way and confessing that it is I that is leading, guiding and directing them.

Woe upon woe! My words have gone forth and they shall not come back to Me void.

What is left for Me to do? Tell Me, My children, what is left to do.

You have forsaken the one and only living God and you have made your own Gods. You have plowed deep the furloughs of evil and you sow wild seeds continually. Your harvest is now coming forth and it will truly set your teeth on edge, saith the One and Only True God. I have spoken and so shall it be.

Jeremiah 31:30 (NIV)
Instead, everyone will die for their own sin; whoever eats sour grapes—their own teeth will be set on edge.

Everlasting chains of judgment await those who would not yield to My wooing and My warnings.

I tried to not touch the American shores, but America would not repent entirely and completely. She still holds onto her idols thinking that I will not revenge the blood of My Son that ran down Calvary's hill.

This earthquake is another wake up call for **America**, but what is she doing with the wakeup call? There is still another earthquake to come and all will surely know that **Revelation 9** has truly come to light.

Bypass your mind church and walk with Me in complete and total obedience to what I have called you forth to do. Repent and follow Me saith the Father, for I will truly lead you by the still waters in this age of great tribulation.

Revelation 9 (NIV)
The fifth angel sounded his trumpet, and I saw a star that had fallen from the sky to the earth. The star was given the key to the shaft of the Abyss. When he opened the Abyss, smoke rose from it like the smoke from a gigantic furnace. The sun and sky were darkened by the smoke from the Abyss. And out of the smoke locusts came down on the

earth and were given power like that of scorpions of the earth. They were told not to harm the grass of the earth or any plant or tree, but only those people who did not have the seal of God on their foreheads. They were not allowed to kill them but only to torture them for five months. And the agony they suffered was like that of the sting of a scorpion when it strikes. During those days people will seek death but will not find it; they will long to die, but death will elude them.

The locusts looked like horses prepared for battle. On their heads they wore something like crowns of gold, and their faces resembled human faces. Their hair was like women's hair, and their teeth were like lions' teeth. They had breastplates like breastplates of iron, and the sound of their wings was like the thundering of many horses and chariots rushing into battle. They had tails with stingers, like scorpions, and in their tails they had power to torment people for five months. They had as king over them the angel of the Abyss, whose name in Hebrew is Abaddon and in Greek is Apollyon (that is, Destroyer).

The first woe is past; two other woes are yet to come. The sixth angel sounded his trumpet, and I heard a voice coming from the four horns of the golden altar that is before God. It said to the sixth angel who had the trumpet, "Release the four angels who are bound at the great river Euphrates." And the four angels who had been kept ready for this very hour and day and month and year were released to kill a third of mankind. The number of the mounted troops was twice ten thousand times ten thousand. I heard their number.

The horses and riders I saw in my vision looked like this: Their breastplates were fiery red, dark blue, and yellow as sulfur. The heads of the horses resembled the heads of lions, and out of their mouths came fire, smoke and sulfur. A third of mankind was killed by the three plagues of fire, smoke and sulfur that came out of their mouths. The power of the horses was in their mouths and in their tails; for their tails were like snakes, having heads with which they inflict injury.

The rest of mankind who were not killed by these plagues still did not repent of the work of their hands; they did not stop worshiping demons, and idols of gold, silver, bronze, stone and wood—idols that cannot see or hear or walk. Nor did they repent of their murders, their magic arts, their sexual immorality or their thefts.

Aftershock of Sin

First of all little one, I am able to do all things. After all, I am the Great I Am and I created this universe and all things in it, therefore I can take care of it.

You must understand that there is an aftershock in all things. The aftershock of sin holds great recompense. All who willingly sin will have to pay this price, no matter who they are.

The sin nature is running rampant in the **United States**, even at this given time when all My wrath is being poured out upon those who sin. The consequences are so great, but they still love their idols.

I am about to do a new thing in the earth for My church and My church needs to be listening for My voice continually, day and night, and in every given second of the day. I need to give her advice and directions.

At this given hour I say: those who have an ear, let them hear what the Lord is saying to the Body as a whole. For I am still speaking to the Body as a whole. I have not fragmented My church.

At this given time, leagues of angels have been disbursed to do the mighty works that must be done across the land.

I am personally supervising this move across the land. Preparations are being made for My Son to come and gather up My people for the last and final time before the great Armageddon begins. The tribulation will be intense and the peoples will run to and fro and many will die for lack of faith.

I have spoken and said build up your most holy faith, but the church has not heeded My warnings. It is time to get in the battle and fight according to My battle plans, and not the enemies. I have spoken to My people and said praise Me! But My people have not heeded that warning either.

Just as Joshua marched around the walls of Jericho and gave a mighty shout of praise, and My Holy Angels caused the walls of Jericho to Fall, the same will happen as My people begin to praise Me.

Joshua did not raise a sword, for Praise was his perfected weapon. Learn to praise Me in all things. Do not speak of the problem; just give it to Me in praise.

I taught My servant Merle Crothers about praise (oh so many years ago) and he has been instructing My people to praise Me, but that seems to easy, so My people continue to contend with their own strength and they fail every time. Perfected praise is where it is at.

The harvest of sin has begun and people will not be able to stand the harvest. Their sins are many and they have come up to My nostrils as a great stench and I am causing them to reap what they have sown. At this given time many will curse Me and fall away, for they will not repent still, and I have no other recourse, but to continue the harvest of their sins.

Many who stand before Me and say Lord, Lord. Will be cast into the great abyss, for they are wolves in sheep clothing. Still others, who are afraid to stand before Me and say Lord, will be plucked out of the eternal flames and will be washed pure as snow and be used mightily in My Kingdom Authority.

> **Jude 22-23 (NIV)**
> Be merciful to those who doubt; 23 save others by snatching them from the fire; to others show mercy, mixed with fear—hating even the clothing stained by corrupted flesh.

My church must not faint at this given time. (The wilderness experience is about over,) and great salvation is about to come over the church. Still a little longer, then My Great Glory shall cover the land, and many souls will be brought into the Kingdom and many great signs, wonders and miracles will occur.

The next seven years will be a time of great conquest for the church. My everlasting arm will be seen all across the continent. All who have eyes to see and ears to hear will know this movement is truly of Me and that I am doing what I have promised throughout the ages.

I am calling for all My children to come up higher and take a seat in the heavenly throne room of My presence and be taught of the Lord in this end time hour. For great will be the instructions from My throne. My people will need to hear My instructions to survive in this great battle that will come upon this land.

Wash the eyes with My eye salve. Cleanse the mouth with My great anointing from upon high. Open the ears to the call from heaven and close them to the call from the world. Great and mighty will be the salvation of those who truly have ears to hear and eyes to see what is going on in the spirit realm.

Many are still running to and fro. They will not believe the reports of My prophets and they are being sucked into the system of the evil one and they are giving themselves over to seducing spirits and they shall perish saith your Father.

Conclusion

It is my sincere hope that as you have read these prophecies you will gain a greater sense of what God is going to be doing in these End Times. We cannot pretend any longer that God is not serious. He is about His business and He is performing His agenda.

There is no good thing that He will withhold from those who love Him and are following Him with all of their hearts. It is important to know what God is doing and you cannot go around like an ostrich. You have to have to be in the Spirit at all times and this collection of prophecies demonstrate just how far God will go to bring His people back to Him.

I encourage you to not wait until the last call has been made. Heed the warnings that have come through God's prophetic voice. Know that everything that can be shaken will be shaken because God has said that He is gonna shake this earth with earthquakes. The time has come for us to reap the bad seeds that we have sowed so that God can prune us, change us and rearrange us for His Glory.

While there is gonna be destruction on all sides and in all ways we have a promise from the Father that He will bring Revival and cause the hearts of men, women, boys & girls to change for Him. Even so come Lord Jesus.

About Pastor/Evangelist Barbara Lynch
The Lighthouse Inc., Church.

The Father has chosen her to be an Evangelist, Revivalist and Glory Carrier for Him. Her heart's desire is to please her Father in Heaven. She is committed to staying before Him and seeking His face at every moment.

Pst. Barbara walks under many anointings and has carried forth and completed many assignments for the Lord.

No stranger to pain and suffering herself, Pst. Barbara has a heart for children and those who are down and out. She has compassion for the lost and dying of this world and she loves to minister to God's people. She practices love at every level and teaches others to do the same.

It is in service to God's people; ministering, mentoring, leading and encouraging them to seek the deeper depths of the Father that she allows the Father to use her with complete abandon. Selfless, caring, willing to go to any length to reach the hearts of the Father's people, she has laid her life down for Jesus, her true friend.

The Holy Spirit would teach her everything that she would need to know. The Father led Pst. Barbara to open a Church called "Haven of Rest" in her home in 1984. As the Fathers plans grew, and the Father expanded the ministry from "Haven of Rest" to the "Lighthouse Church Inc". in 1991. She has been instrumental in fulfilling the call to equip the Saints of God to do the work of the Father. Because she allowed the Father to train her in His ways she has led many to His throne of Grace.

She is mentoring those who have a heart to be in the ministry. She is a forerunner. Pst. Barbara has a powerful deliverance ministry where many captives are being set free. She is actively working to set God's people free through deliverance. Pst. Barbara leads a small band of committed warriors who love the Lord. She is committed to teaching and training the Body of Christ to walk in the gifts of the Spirit.

As the Father leads Pst. Barbara is accepting speaking engagements. For more information call (302) 697-1472. She is located at 6 South Railroad Avenue; Wyoming, DE 19934-1026. You may follow her ministry at www.lighthousechurchinc.org

www.ingramcontent.com/pod-product-compliance
Lightning Source LLC
Chambersburg PA
CBHW031207090426
42736CB00009B/820